CROWNING GLORY

Hats off to Black hair in all its glory. And to the Crown Act movement
for advocating laws to protect the right to wear natural hair
with pride and without discrimination.

CBW

From press and curl to sister locs, this book is dedicated to the people who've made
magic with my hair—hairdressers, barbers, locticians, and around-the-way beauticians
Miss Minnie, Ms. Mary Ware, and Ms. Audrey Aduama—with a special shout-out to
Beau Nubian Brummel in Roxbury, MA, for my first glorious afro.

EH

Text copyright © 2024 by Carole Boston Weatherford
Illustrations copyright © 2024 by Ekua Holmes

First edition 2024

Library of Congress Catalog Card Number 2024930404
ISBN 978-0-7636-9794-5

24 25 26 27 28 29 FRS 10 9 8 7 6 5 4 3 2 1

Printed in Altona, Manitoba, Canada

This book was typeset in Avenir.
The illustrations were done in mixed-media collage and acrylic on paper.

Candlewick Press
99 Dover Street
Somerville, Massachusetts 02144

www.candlewick.com

CROWNING GLORY

A CELEBRATION OF BLACK HAIR

Carole Boston Weatherford

illustrated by **Ekua Holmes**

CANDLEWICK PRESS

There came a moment in the course of time when all the planets must have been aligned.

And the sun was proudly beaming down
on Africa's daughters, all wearing crowns.

Five queens from around the world
rocking afros and flowing curls.

But we don't need pageants to declare our reigns.
Majesty is woven into our manes.

Our hair is a lioness, born to be wild.
We pride ourselves on flair and style.

Our hair is frizzy, strong and free,
with roots as deep as an ebony tree.

Cornrows forming complex patterns:
zigzags, curves, or rings like Saturn's.

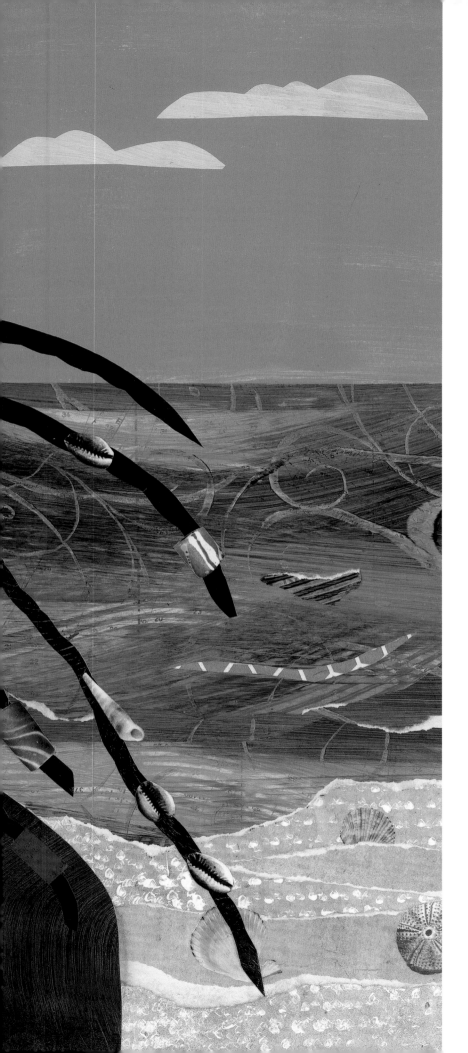

Shells and beads on boxy braids.

Like waterfalls, our hair cascades.

A flowery 'fro that's wash and go,
showered with shea for a glossy glow.

A sun-kissed halo that springs and fluffs
is twice as nice parted into puffs.

Pigtails, space buns, ponytail,
an updo swirly as a snail.

A regal pouf that scrapes the sky,
finger waves that look so fly.

Bantu knots and flowing locs,
braided mohawks and 'fro-hawks.

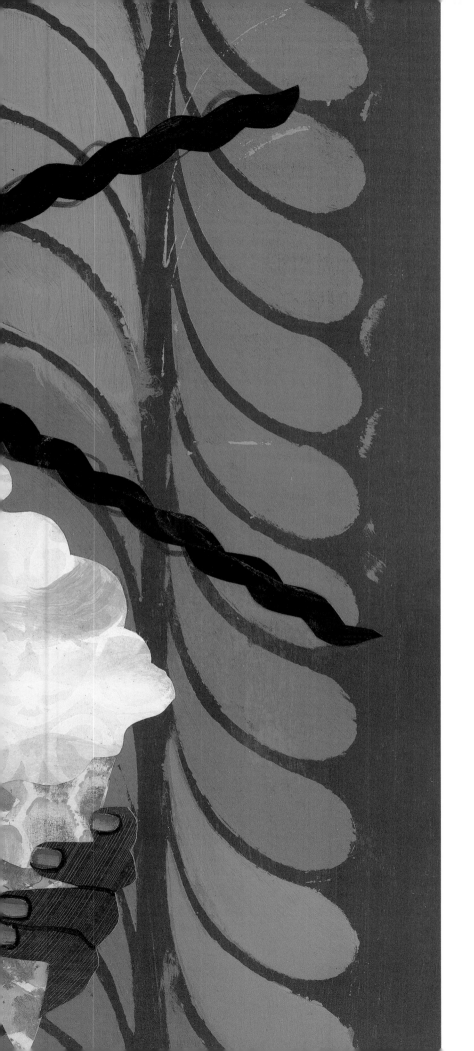

Two-strand,
  three-strand,
    twirly twists,

  edges laid in baby hair wisps.

To heed beliefs or cheer gray days,
hijabs, hats, headwraps, geles.

Saturdays, a sleek silk press
bound with bows for Sunday best.

A ritual of hand and heart,
each stunning head a work of art.
Each royal coil coaxed by kin.
Each strand a story without end.

GLOSSARY

afro ('fro): a tightly curled hairstyle that stands up and out, in a circle around the head

baby hair: short hair growing around the front of the hairline

Bantu knots: twisted braids formed into small circular knots; named after African peoples originating in central and southern Africa

boxy braid: a style in which the hair is plaited into square cylinders, using four strands of hair for each plait

braid/plait: a single length of hair made up of strands wrapped around one another

coil: a curly style created by twisting hair around the finger, creating a spiral

cornrows: hair braided very close to the scalp, usually in rows or a pattern. Cornrows were used to hide seeds and rice that kidnapped Africans brought with them to grow food in the Americas; they were also designed to serve as maps to teach others how to escape north to freedom.

crown: a jeweled headpiece worn by a ruler; the top of the head; a fancy hat, especially when worn to church

crowning glory: one's hair

ebony tree: a tree that produces valuable black wood

finger wave: a way to set wet hair, using the fingers to create curves in the hair

five queens: In 2019, Black women made history as the titleholders of five major beauty pageants: Nia Franklin (New York) as Miss America; Cheslie Kryst (North Carolina) as Miss USA; Zozibini Tunzi (South Africa) as Miss Universe; Toni-Ann Singh (Jamaica) as Miss World; and Kaliegh Garris (Connecticut) as Miss Teen USA.

frizzy: composed of small, tight curls of different textures

'fro: *see* afro

'fro-hawk: a mohawk with an afro as the longer hair down the center of the head

gele: a headscarf worn in many parts of Africa

headwrap: a piece of cloth fastened to the head by knotting the cloth ends together

hijab: a head covering worn by some Muslim women

locs: (also called dread locs or dreads): braids formed by twisting hair into sections that look like rope

mane: a full head of hair

mohawk: a hairstyle with hair on both sides of the head worn, or cut, close to the scalp, leaving a longer strip of hair down the center of the head

pigtails: two braids plaited on either side of the head

plait: *see* braid/plait

ponytail: longer hair pulled back and tied down at the back, creating a strand of hair falling down the neck

pouf: hair rolled backward into a pile on the top of the forehead

press: a way to straighten hair using a metal comb heated inside a small oven or over a gas stove burner

puffs: a hairstyle in which the hair is tied into a ball shape, either on the sides or at the top of the head

shea: an African nut butter used as a lotion, salve, and moisturizer

space buns: hair that is styled into two buns like those worn by Princess Leia in the 1977 film *Star Wars*

strand: a single piece, length, or section of hair

three-strand twist: a style in which the hair is split into three sections, which are wrapped around one another to create one plait

twirly twists: a style in which the hair is braided with colorful yarns

two-strand twist: a style in which the hair is split into two sections, which are wrapped around each other to create one plait

updo: hair that is pinned up and off of the face, held in place with bobby pins, barrettes, or combs